T0021989

queens of STEAM

Dr. Kizzmekia Corbett

The Virologist Who Changed the World

by Mari Bolte

9781223187501 English Hardcover
9781223187518 English Paperback
9781223187525 English eBook

Published by Paw Prints Publishing
PawPrintsPublishing.com
Printed in Canada

See the Glossary on page 29 for definitions of words found in **bold** in the text!

"People are going to try and tell you who you should be. You have to remember who you are at all times."

–Dr. Kizzmekia Corbett

Dr. Kizzmekia Corbett is a scientist. She studies how the body responds to **viruses**.

Saving the Day with Science

It's January 2020. The city of Wuhan, China, is on lockdown. People are getting sick. Many are dying. No one knows the cause.

Soon, the cause is discovered. It is a **disease** called COVID-19 (coronavirus disease 2019). By March, the disease has spread across the globe. No one knows what to do or how to stop it. The world needs a scientist to help! Enter Dr. Kizzmekia Corbett.

Wuhan is a large city in Central China. COVID-19 started there and quickly spread across the world.

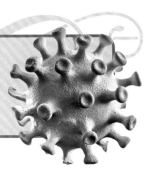

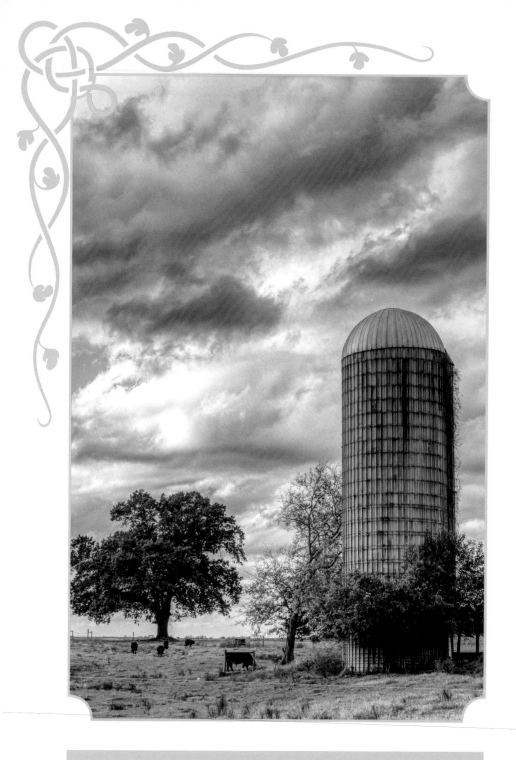

Dr. Kizzmekia grew up in a rural part of northern North Carolina.

The "Queen" of Biomedical Research

Dr. Kizzmekia Shanta Corbett was born on January 26, 1986. She grew up with her mother, stepfather, stepsiblings, and a number of **foster siblings** in the small North Carolina town of Hillsborough.

Even small kingdoms create great queens.

The "Kizz" in Dr. Kizzmekia (Kizz–ME–key–uh) comes from the character Kizzy in the 1976 book *Roots.* Dr. Kizzmekia's mom added "mekia" as her own creative touch.

Young Dr. Kizzmekia was kind. One day, she asked her mom if a friend could live with them. This friend had a bad homelife and nowhere else to go after school. This friend would be the first of many foster children the Corbetts welcomed into their home.

Dr. Kizzmekia knew she wanted a career that would allow her to help people. Her dream was to become the first Black woman to win the **Nobel Prize** in Medicine. Her fourth-grade teacher, Ms. Bradsher, encouraged that dream.

"Queen" Curie

Marie Curie was the first woman to win a Nobel Prize. She is also the only woman to win twice. Curie studied radioactivity, the energy that comes from certain **elements**. X-rays and other medical tools use radioactive elements. Her work was used to save lives.

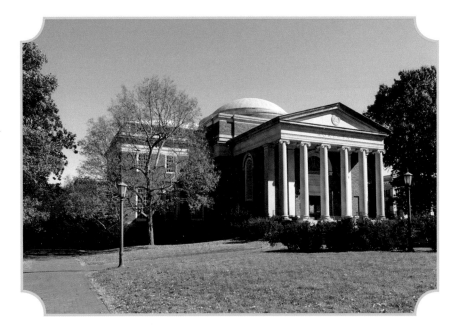

Dr. Kizzmekia's internship was at the University of North Carolina, Chapel Hill, for two summers during high school.

When Dr. Kizzmekia was old enough to work, she got an **internship** with a program called Project SEED. Project SEED gives low-income students real-life **STEAM** experiences. They get to work with scientists and in research labs. Now, she could finally ask questions and get answers from real scientists.

More than 12,000 students have been a part of Project SEED. It started in 1968. It is run by the American Chemical Society.

In 2004, Dr. Kizzmekia got a full **scholarship** to the University of Maryland, Baltimore County. She was part of the Meyerhoff Scholars Program, which supports minority students who want to earn advanced degrees in STEAM. Professors noted her hard work and enthusiasm.

As a student, Dr. Kizzmekia studied a type of **bacteria** that causes scarlet fever in humans. She also worked as a **lab technician**. In 2006, she spent the summer working at the National Institutes of Health (NIH). There, she got to know scientist Dr. Barney Graham.

When Dr. Kizzmekia first met Dr. Graham, he asked what she wanted to do. She looked him straight in the eye and said, "I want your job." Go, Dr. Kizzmekia!

Dr. Kizzmekia studied biological sciences and sociology. Both subjects are part of the "S" or "Science" in STEAM.

Dr. Kizzmekia finished college in 2008. She was the first person in her family to earn a four-year degree. She continued summer work at the NIH until 2009. But her education wasn't yet complete. A doctoral degree, or PhD, was next. After all, "doctor" had a nice sound to it!

More than 30,000 students attend the
University of North Carolina, Chapel Hill.

The Road to Royalty:
Becoming Dr. Corbett

Dr. Kizzmekia pursued her doctoral degree at the University of North Carolina, Chapel Hill. There, she studied dengue fever, a disease that is spread by tropical mosquitoes. There are no medicines or **vaccines** to fight it. Dr. Kizzmekia wanted to know how it affected children.

There have been many biomedical science "Queens of STEAM" throughout history. Mary Wortley Montagu worked on smallpox vaccines in the 1700s!

Dr. Kizzmekia saw that not everyone has the same response to viruses and vaccines. Understanding these differences can help scientists find solutions that work for everyone.

Tools of a "Virologist Queen"

Virologists study viruses that affect living things. They learn to identify, treat, and prevent those viruses. There are many tools of the trade that make their work easier.

- Test tubes are used to grow and study how viruses change over time.
- Microscopes make tiny bacteria and viruses large enough to be seen.
- Polymerase chain reaction (PCR) machines can quickly make many copies of small pieces of DNA. They help scientists detect diseases and create vaccines.
- Autoclaves use steam to clean lab equipment.

In 2014, Dr. Kizzmekia earned her PhD in microbiology and immunology, and Dr. Graham gave her a job at the NIH. There, she studied vaccines for two different **coronaviruses**. One was severe acute respiratory syndrome (SARS). The other was Middle East respiratory syndrome (MERS). There was a SARS outbreak from 2002 to 2003. MERS was first reported in 2012.

The NIH started out as a one-room lab in the late 1800s. Now, it is a cutting-edge medical research center.

There are many types
of coronaviruses overall.
Some are mild. Others
are deadly. Most people
get *some* form of a coronavirus during
their lifetime. The virus spreads through
coughing, sneezing, and touching.

At 6 a.m. on December 31, 2019, Dr. Kizzmekia
received an email from Dr. Graham. "Get
ready for 2020," he wrote. There was
a new coronavirus in town. And it was
causing COVID-19.

Dr. Kizzmekia is often invited to events to speak about her life and
work, including the Joanna Coles Power 100 Luncheon in 2021.

COVID Timeline

December 2019: The first cases of COVID-19 are reported in Wuhan, China.

March 2020: A cruise ship docks in San Francisco, California. Passengers onboard are sick with COVID-19.

March 2020: The world shuts down. Schools close, and people start working from home.

June 2020: US states begin to reopen. Cases then skyrocket.

January 2021: The United States sets a record for COVID-19 deaths, with a week of more than 3,300 each day.

Late 2022–early 2023: A "tripledemic" of COVID-19, influenza, and respiratory syncytial virus (RSV) circulates through the United States.

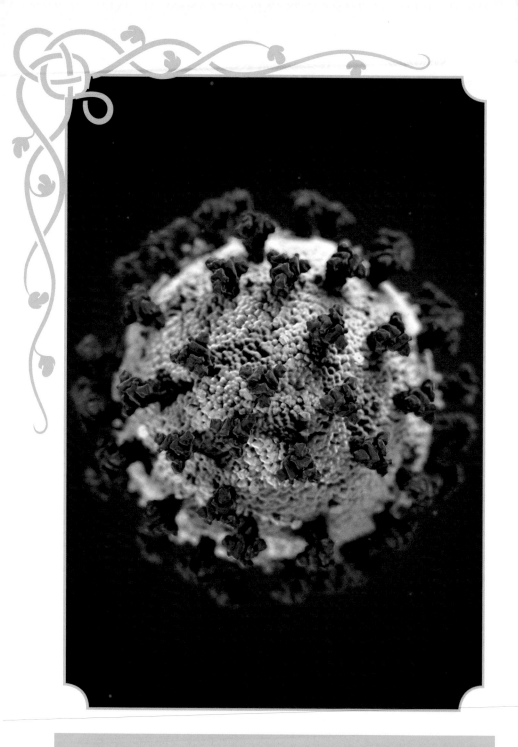

A COVID-19 molecule is extremely small. It can be seen only under special microscopes, such as scanning electron microscopes.

The "Queen" vs. The Crown

It can take a long time to create a vaccine. But scientists around the world used their combined knowledge about coronaviruses to build one together quickly. COVID-19 was similar to SARS. Everything Dr. Kizzmekia had already learned would come in handy.

Coronaviruses are covered with **proteins**. The proteins look like a spiky crown. This is what gives the virus its name. In Latin, *corona* means "crown."

Dr. Kizzmekia led a team of scientists. They worked with a company called Moderna. Moderna specializes in **mRNA** research. Dr. Kizzmekia's team worked with mRNA to create the next generation of vaccines, one of which would help with the COVID-19 outbreak.

How Does mRNA Work?

mRNA was first found in the 1960s. By the 1970s, scientists saw that mRNA could carry vaccines into cells. Cells make up all living things. The vaccine tells cells in the body to make antibodies. The antibodies then fight disease. The mRNA breaks down once its job is done. COVID-19 shots are the first mRNA vaccines used on the general public.

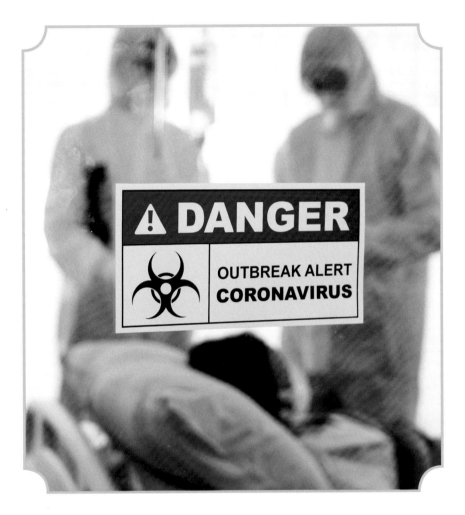

In 2020, more than 20 million Americans tested positive for COVID-19.

A vaccine seemed so far off. But it was the only way to reopen the world. Dr. Kizzmekia felt the pressure. Her team continued to work quickly on a vaccine that would be reliable. Their work would save countless lives.

In March 2020, President Donald Trump and Dr. Anthony Fauci visited the NIH. Dr. Kizzmekia gave them a tour. President Trump asked her questions and looked at the work her team had done thus far. Three days later, he signed a bill into law. That bill set aside $8.3 billion for emergency COVID-19 relief. Around $3 billion of that went to testing vaccines, vaccine creation, and treatment.

In 2022, a clue on *Jeopardy* read, "Dr. Kizzmekia Corbett led the team that came up with the COVID-19 vaccine from this company founded in 2010."

Dr. Kizzmekia hosted President Joe Biden and Dr. Fauci at her lab in 2021.

Ten days after this bill was signed, the team began clinical trials on a testable vaccine from Dr. Kizzmekia's team. It was the fastest development of a vaccine ever. Dr. Kizzmekia made sure the people who took part in the trials were from different backgrounds. It was important that all people were represented, no matter their age or race.

At the time, there were more than 140 different treatments and vaccines being worked on and tested. The first ever vaccine for COVID-19 was given to a nurse in New York on December 14, 2020. This vaccine was made by Pfizer, a competitor of Moderna, the company Dr. Kizzmekia was working with. The Moderna vaccine was ready just a week after the Pfizer vaccine. Six million doses were shipped around the country. They had Dr. Kizzmekia's royal seal of approval.

Dr. Kizzmekia spoke at the 2022 Massachusetts Conference for Women, where speakers discuss "issues that matter most to women."

The Crown Lives On

Dr. Kizzmekia was showered with awards for her part in the Moderna COVID-19 vaccine. She also received many new job offers. In 2021, she and her fiancé, Lumas Helaire, moved to Boston so she could take a job offer at the Harvard T. H. Chan School of Public Health. Being prepared for the next pandemic is now at the top of her to-do list!

In 2020, Dr. Kizzmekia described herself in an interview. The "queen" proclaimed, "I am Christian. I'm Black. I am Southern, I'm an **empath**. I'm feisty, sassy, and fashionable."

Dr. Kizzmekia had many good mentors and teachers. Now, *she* is the mentor. She believes that everyone should feel like they belong in her court. "It's important that people not only feel as though they belong in the lab but also that their voice is heard," she has said. Every year, she speaks at conferences, addressing the next "queens" of STEAM.

Her hometown of Hillsborough, North Carolina, has declared January 12, 2021, Dr. Kizzmekia "Kizzy" Corbett Day.

The field of science can be high-pressure. But Dr. Kizzmekia knows young people can handle it. They just need to be prepared.

"If you think you're interested [in STEAM], you just have to start," she has said. "There are internship programs, there are scholarship programs, there are shadowing programs . . . that can help you get your feet wet." First, find out if you like it. Learn all you can. Then, go for it!

Dr. Kizzmekia hasn't won the Nobel Prize—yet. But there's still plenty of time!

Quiz

1. COVID-19 reached the United States in:
   A. December 2020

   B. December 2019

   C. January 2020

   D. May 2021

2. An mRNA vaccine tells the body to make:
   A. proteins

   B. antibodies

   C. disease

   D. both B and C

3. Dr. Kizzmekia's first job was:
   A. an internship at a science lab

   B. flipping burgers

   C. a personal assistant

   D. a virologist

4. Dr. Kizzmekia specializes in:
   A. the common cold and COVID-19

   B. microbiology and immunology

   C. lab work and virology

   D. grant writing and virus response

Key: 1) C; 2) B; 3) A; 4) B

Glossary

bacteria (bak-TEER-ee-uh): a group of single-celled organisms; some can cause infections and illness in living things

coronaviruses (kuh-ROW-nuh-vai-ruhs-ehz): groups of viruses that cause illness in birds and mammals

disease (dih-ZEEZ): a sickness

elements (EHL-uh-muhnts): basic substances that cannot be broken down into smaller parts or changed

empath (EM-path): a person who finds it easy to recognize and understand how others are feeling

foster siblings (FAW-stuhr SIB-lihngz): children without homes that are hosted by a family for a period of time

internship (IN-turn-ship): work experience offered to students that gives them on-the-job training for future careers

lab technician (LAB tek-NIh-shun): someone who helps scientists with research, testing, and experiments

mRNA (EM-arr-en-aye): called "messenger RNA," a group of acids that move information within cells

Nobel Prize (no-BEL PRYZE): an annual prize awarded to people who have done important work in the sciences and literature, and in the pursuit of peace

proteins (PROH-teenz): substances found in all living things that help the body function properly

scholarship (SKAAL-ur-ship): an award given to students to help pay for their education

STEAM (STEEM): the fields of Science, Technology, Engineering, Arts, and Mathematics; virology is part of science

vaccines (vak-SEENZ): medicines

viruses (VAI-ruh-suhz): tiny organisms that can infect cells and cause sickness

Spread the Word, Not the Germs

COVID-19 affected everyone's life. Another pandemic might do the same thing. Pick a subject from the list below and then create a poster to share what you've learned.

- How does a virus infect a person?
- How does a virus spread?
- How do people fight the spread of a virus?
- What is COVID-19?
- How do coronavirus vaccines work?
- Where in the world fought COVID-19 the best? How did they do it?
- What was the timeline of COVID-19 from the first case to today?

ACTIVITY

It's Time to Celebrate!

Dr. Kizzmekia Corbett isn't the only scientist with an official day. Celebrate Scientists Day is every year on March 14. That's Albert Einstein's birthday. Even if it's not March yet, you can spread the word about amazing scientific advancements—and the scientists behind them.

- Choose a scientist. (Dr. Kizzmekia is a great place to start!)
- When did they live? Where? Learn more about their lives and how they became interested in STEAM.
- What field do they work in? How do they use STEAM every day?
- How have they contributed to the world of science?
- What would the world be like without their contribution?
- Use what you've learned to create a presentation to share with others. Draw a poster or create a slideshow. Make a pamphlet, build a diorama, or write a speech.

Index